# Whisky Cask Investment

*Look after the whisky, and the whisky will look after you.*

# Whisky Cask Investment

## Building Wealth Through Whisky Casks

*Fiona Rintoul*

SPINK

First published in 2022 by Spink and Son Ltd



ISBN 978-1-912667-90-1

Typeset by Russell Whittle

Printed and bound in Malta by Gutenberg Press Ltd

Spink and Son Ltd
69 Southampton Row
London WC1B 4ET

www.spinkbooks.com

# CONTENTS


| | | |
|---|---|---|
| CHAPTER 1 | INTRODUCTION | 1 |
| CHAPTER 2 | A STELLAR PERFORMER | 11 |
| CHAPTER 3 | A HISTORY OF WHISKY CASK INVESTMENT | 21 |
| CHAPTER 4 | THE LIFE CYCLE OF A CASK | 33 |
| CHAPTER 5 | HOW TO CHOOSE YOUR CASK | 45 |
| CHAPTER 6 | BUILDING WEALTH THROUGH WHISKY CASKS | 61 |
| CHAPTER 7 | FUTURE DIRECTIONS IN WHISKY CASK INVESTMENT | 75 |
| APPENDICES | THE DISTILLERIES OF SCOTLAND | 85 |

# INTRODUCTION

Which investment can offer stable 10-12% annual returns regardless of market turbulence? Which investment automatically increases in value as time passes? Which investment is almost completely uncorrelated with global financial markets? The answer is whisky casks.

Like every other industry, the whisky industry experiences peaks and troughs. The price of whisky can fluctuate over time like that of any other commodity. However, whisky casks have one unique attribute that makes them different from every other type of investment. Because whiskies with older age statements command higher prices than younger spirits, the value of whisky casks appreciates over time as the spirit contained in them matures. Barring a complete global collapse in the consumption of single-malt Scotch whisky, investing in a whisky cask can be a bit like locking a bar of silver away for 10 years and receiving a bar of gold at the end.

# Enhance your own returns

Managed professional investment in whisky casks is comparatively new, with a history of at most 10 years, but whisky insiders have understood the value of whisky casks for centuries. For investing in a whisky cask doesn't just give you access to an asset that automatically appreciates provided there is demand for single-malt whisky; it also provides you with an investment that you can curate to increase its value.

Aside from property, which can be done up and sold for a profit, there are few assets that you can manage and improve to maximise your returns. With whisky casks, a broker can advise you on how to finish the spirit in your cask to create a unique whisky that will command a high price from one of the many independent bottlers that purchases rare and speciality single-malt whisky casks.

Independent bottlers form a larger part of the whisky industry than many people realise. In 2016, 58% of whisky expressions on the market were independent bottlings. Typically, these bottlings are 20-30% more expensive than original bottlings, catering to the higher end of the whisky market.

The possibilities offered by cask management make whisky casks a flexible investment. You can choose how you curate your cask to suit both your own monetisation timescale and market trends. Of course, monetisation depends on an available buyer, but the large number of independent bottlers in the market and the premium they can charge for unusual and interesting bottlings increase the chances of finding a buyer.

Whisky cask investment is unique in another way too. You can enjoy it. Not only can you bottle your own cask if you choose, keeping some or all of the bottles for your own consumption or to use as gifts, you can enjoy visiting your cask and sampling your spirit as it matures and can be involved in deciding how best to curate it.

# Scotch whisky: simply the best

Scotland is not the only country in the world that produces whisky, but the quality and variety of Scotch whisky is unrivalled. Like whisky itself, deep heritage, mastery of craft and the highest professional standards take time to produce. Whisky has been distilled in Scotland for at least six centuries and probably much longer.

Today, the Scotch whisky industry is more vibrant than ever. Scotland has 138 operating distilleries, with some 22 million casks maturing in Scottish warehouses. In 2021, Scotch whisky exports were worth £4.5bn, accounting for 75% of Scottish and 22% of UK food and drink exports. This book's focus is therefore Scotch whisky distilleries. Nowhere else in the world can you find the breadth and depth of product that exists in the Scotch whisky industry. If you want to start investing in whisky casks, Scotland is indisputably the best embarkation point for that journey.

# A professionalising investment sector

This book equips you with everything you need to know to get started in whisky cask investment. It reveals the criteria to consider when choosing your whisky cask and examines how you can build wealth with a single whisky cask or a portfolio of casks.

The book also delves into the history of whisky cask investment, concentrating on the years since 2014 which have seen a rapid professionalisation of the whisky cask investment sector. With professionalisation has come transparency and robust analytics. In this book, we introduce you to the statistics underlying whisky cask investment returns and to the BC20 index. This was created by Braeburn Whisky and is the first index of whisky casks.

Whisky cask investment is at a turning point. Whisky casks are increasingly being sold at auction, boosting price transparency, and professional investors such as wealth managers and family offices are beginning to look at investing in the sector. This book aims to help you to understand an investment that can be both lucrative and fun, facilitating access to an uncorrelated asset class that is open to almost everyone and can lend stability to your wider investment portfolio.

# 2

# A STELLAR PERFORMER:

The great differentiator between whisky casks and other real assets such as works of art or collectible bottles of whisky is that, regardless of market movements, the value of the spirit within a whisky cask does not remain the same through time. Instead, as the spirit matures it becomes more valuable. A cask bought today will be a different product and will almost certainly carry a higher price tag in three years' time. This unique circumstance has helped underpin stable returns from whisky casks during varying market conditions.

# Supply and demand

Over the past 10-15 years, the changing dynamics of the whisky industry have also buoyed the performance of whisky cask investments. As whisky has become a premium drink, with whisky drinkers increasingly prizing single-malt whiskies over the blends that have traditionally formed the industry's backbone, demand for old, rare and unusual whisky casks has grown.

Historical factors also play a role. The so-called whisky loch that came into being after a period of over-production in the 1970s led to distillery closures when the market slumped in the 1980s. Rare casks from the 1980s now sell at a premium, particularly those from the iconic distilleries that were closed by Diageo's predecessor, the Distillers Company Limited. Top of the list is the much-lamented Port Ellen distillery on Islay, which is due to restart production in 2023 after refurbishment.

Demand for single-malt whisky now outstrips supply by a considerable margin. Due to the nature of whisky production, increased demand cannot easily be met with increased supply. Yes, distilleries can switch to running at full capacity, but once full capacity is reached, it is difficult to increase production further.

If a distillery wants to push production to a new level, it needs to introduce one or more new stills, which is far from straightforward. Because of the many new whisky distilleries that have been opening in Scotland in recent years, coppersmiths such as the famous Forsyths in Forres typically have a backlog of orders. This has led some whisky distilleries to look beyond Scotland for stills to coppersmiths such as FRILLI Srl in Siena.

Even when a coppersmith with capacity can be found, the problems are not over for a distillery wishing to expand production. Any new stills must have all the idiosyncrasies associated with the existing stills to ensure consistency of output. If the spirit changes, this can impact the distillery's reputation.

OLD STYLE SOUR MASH
BOURBON WHISKEY

## New markets

As a result, Scotch whisky distilleries are struggling to meet demand for single malt. Many have dropped age statements from their whiskies, as they try to rebuild their inventories. Older core expressions, such as the Lagavulin 16-year-old, have become harder to find.

Most single-malt whisky currently produced in Scotland is bottled by the time it is 15 years old and often much sooner. This generates further demand for older and rarer spirits.

Of course, future demand is never guaranteed, and there have been dips in whisky's popularity in the past, resulting in unsold spirit and distillery closures. Nowadays, however, demand for whisky comes from a more diverse range of sources, promoting stability.

New consumers, such as women and younger people, now complement the stereotypical whisky drinker: an older man in a tweed jacket with a dog at his feet. In addition, new markets with huge potential are opening up, for example in Asia and South America.

India is now the second largest importer of Scotch whisky in the world, and opportunities to expand the market for Scotch whisky in India are considerable. Currently, Scotch whisky accounts for just 2% of the Indian market, where domestic whisky production is well established. Most of that goes for blend, but there is a growing market for statement single-malt whiskies among the emerging middle classes.

Overall, analysts expect sales of Scotch whisky in India to surge in the coming years on the back of an anticipated sharp drop in tariffs as part of a UK-India trade deal. This could take Scotch whisky to a projected 6% of the total Indian market.

Where consumers go, investors shall follow. Some of the biggest ticket whisky cask sales in recent years have been in China. In 2021, Europe represented 70.1% of whisky cask investment and Asia just 21.7%. However, more Asian investors are expected to enter the whisky cask investment market in the future, boosting both valuations and liquidity.

# Growing data transparency

Increased demand for single-malt whisky and the constraints on supply mean that cask values have been rising. For investors, whisky casks offer a winning combination of resilience to market shocks – the value of whisky casks typically isn't affected by volatility on the stock markets or even geopolitical crises – and the promise of superior returns.

Being uncorrelated to financial markets, whisky casks can also function as a hedge against inflation, as we re-enter an inflationary environment. There is no such thing as an inflation-proof investment, but supply constraints, consumer trends and the alchemy of the whisky maturation process mean whisky casks come close.

In addition, there are tax benefits to investing in whisky casks. Because some of the spirit in the cask evaporates over time – the so-called 'angel's share' – whisky casks are viewed as a wasting asset by the UK tax authority, HMRC.

As a result, whisky casks do not attract capital gains tax when sold, provided they remain in a bonded warehouse.

It is now easier than ever to quantify whisky cask investment returns and to compare whisky casks with other investments. For four years, Braeburn Whisky has been collecting and analysing data on cask valuations by region, age, distillery and other variables. Using these data, the company has created an algorithm that allows it to predict how a specific cask of whisky will appreciate on an annual basis and to back-check those predictions.

The algorithm is calculated using a matrix of real and estimated data points for different distilleries. Since Braeburn Whisky started calculating the algorithm, it has collected almost 5,500 real data points. Estimated data points are calculated by extrapolating from previous or equivalent data. Distilleries with fewer than 10 real data points are excluded from the matrix, as are outlier data. With more data becoming available internally and from whisky cask auctions, the algorithm becomes more precise and easier to verify with each passing year.

An overview of the data is available in the bi-annual Whisky Cask Market Report, which traces the development of whisky cask valuations and puts them in context. Based on the proprietary Braeburn Whisky algorithm, the projected increase in value of Scottish whisky casks in 2021 was 13.1% - evidence of whisky casks' resilience to global shocks.

Braeburn Whisky has also created the BC20 index, the first index of whisky casks. Based on a representative selection of 20 casks of varying ages from different distilleries and regions, the index helps capture the special qualities of whisky casks as an asset class. Unlike other commodities, whisky casks are all unique and the change in their value over time is not just down to economics but also to the maturation of the spirit within them.

In 2021, the projected value of the BC20 index rose by 14.5% - outperforming both traditional stock market indices and gold. Over the four years since the index was created, it has consistently outperformed other asset classes, with the exception of mid to late 2018 when it dipped beneath gold. It also typically outperforms the wider whisky cask market, demonstrating the added value that cask management and diversification can bring.

A portfolio of £100,000 invested in whisky casks in the BC20 index in July 2018 had a projected value of £184,797 at the end of 2021. This outstrips other more traditional asset classes. The S&P 500 index generated £164,264 over the same period and gold £150,242, while the FTSE and the Hang Seng were in negative territory at the end of the review period.

# 3

# A HISTORY OF WHISKY CASK INVESTMENT

People have probably bought whisky casks privately since the dawn of the whisky industry. They may not have conceived of their purchase as an investment, but if they later sold the cask back to the distillery or to a bottler at a profit, it was a form of investment.

Looked at like that, whisky cask investment is as old as the whisky industry itself, which begs the question: how old is the whisky industry? It is impossible to say with any certainty.

Whisky production is an ancient practice probably connected with the northwards spread of Christianity and the lack of grapes to make wine in chillier climes. Some sources suggest that whisky distillation came to Scotland with Christian monks, but it may have been an art already familiar to resourceful Celtic farmers – a use for surplus barley.

The first written reference to whisky in Scotland dates from the end of the fifteenth century. In the Scottish Exchequer Rolls for 1494, there is an entry for "eight bolls of malt to Friar John Cor wherewith to make aquavitae".

A boll was a Scottish measure that represented not more than six bushels and was equivalent to about 150kg. Through that notation about Friar John Cor, the water of life – *uisge beatha* in Gaelic – entered the historical record. Perhaps the friar sold some of the casks of whisky he created from those 150kg of malt to private buyers; perhaps he did not. Either way, private cask sales have been part of the fabric of the whisky industry both in Scotland and beyond for a very long time.

# Cask ownership programmes

In the USA in the 1960s and 1970s, it seems to have been possible to own a hogshead of bourbon through something called a warehouse receipt. According to a 1990s' article in the *Chicago Tribune,* warehouse receipts were sold by commercial banks in whiskey-distilling areas of the USA as a hedge against inflation.

The selling banks in the southern US states where bourbon is produced saw this trade as a way of monetising loans that they had granted to small bourbon distilleries. The trade in warehouse receipts dried up when bourbon distilling passed into the hands of a few large corporations that didn't need credit from local banks.

In Scotland too, there is a long tradition of distilleries selling casks to private buyers to smooth cashflow while they wait for their spirit to mature and become saleable. In the past, organisations or wealthy individuals would acquire casks, which, just like the hogsheads of bourbon in the American South, would remain at the distillery. At some point down the line, the distillery would buy the cask back, providing a return to the purchaser. The distillery would then bottle the cask and take advantage of retail margins. In this model, the cask purchasers, who might have connections with the distillery or be whisky insiders, were effectively providing risk finance to the distilleries.

As happened in bourbon production, this model was stymied by the corporatisation of the whisky industry, which reduced the need for this kind of risk finance. However, private cask ownership programmes are still very much part of the Scotch whisky industry. Newer distilleries in private ownership and ones that have reopened after a period in abeyance often use cask ownership programmes both for bridging finance and to build brand.

Some well-established distilleries and distillery owners have cask ownership programmes too, sometimes with an exclusive edge. Diageo, for example, offers invited private clients the opportunity to buy unique and rare casks through its Casks of Distinction programme. The casks are hand-selected by four master blenders from Diageo's portfolio of 28 operating and 15 closed single-malt distilleries in Scotland. When the cask is bottled, each bottle is serialised and hallmarked with the cask owner's signature.

LAPHROAIG

# Managed cask investment

But these private cask ownership programmes are a different beast from professionally managed whisky cask investment that is open to all and aims to provide a decent investment return. Casks bought through a cask ownership programme will typically cost more than those sourced by a broker and might come with fringe benefits, such as privileged access to special bottlings and invitations to events. Often, casks bought directly from a distillery will also come with certain stipulations, such as fixed timeframes, set sell-back prices or obligations to bottle. This makes them more of a lifestyle purchase than an investment.

Responsible and professionally managed investment in whisky casks is a relatively new phenomenon. Its history dates back to around the mid-2010s.

In 2014, the Platinum Whisky Investment Fund became one of the first private equity funds in the world to focus on whisky with a portfolio of rare single-malt Scottish and Japanese whiskies. Targeted at an exclusive clientele, the fund raised US$12 million from high-net-worth investors in mainland China, Hong Kong, Singapore and the UK, 35% of which was invested in ultra-premium casks. These included a number of 30-year-old Macallan sherry casks and several casks from the Diageo Casks of Distinction programme, for example a 1979 Talisker cask and a 1990 Rosebank cask.

The remainder of the fund's assets was invested in around 12,000 bottles. The fund was liquidated as planned in 2021 with proceeds of US$26 million.

Such whisky cask investment schemes as existed before the mid-2010s were typically of dubious probity and were sometimes outright scams. Perhaps the most famous is the Grandtully Distillery scam. In the 1990s, Stephen Jupe of SSI Ltd sold investors 300 barrels of whisky from the Aberfeldy-based distillery, which had closed in 1910, at inflated prices. Unlike the Grandtully Distillery, the whisky barrels did exist but had been bought from a different distillery, which had no part in the deception. In 2004, Jupe was jailed for five years for this £4 million con.

Even today, it is possible to find whisky brokerage firms that promise unrealistic returns from investing in whisky casks, fail to highlight the risks that are inherent in any investment or use unsuitable data – for example, data relating to rare whisky bottle prices – to promote whisky cask investment portfolios.

# Transparency is all

Brokerage firms such as Braeburn Whisky, which was established in 2019, are writing a new chapter in the history of whisky cask investment. For them, as for responsible investment brokers in all sectors, the watchword is transparency. That is underpinned by an unambiguous cask ownership structure and robust analytical tools with clear parameters and assumptions.

Whisky cask auctions have also boosted transparency in the sector. Spink conducted the first whisky cask auction in 2014, selling a 23-year-old Macallan cask to an Asia-based buyer for just under HK$2 million. This ended the tradition of whisky casks being sold exclusively in darkened rooms in Scotland to whisky insiders. Spink has since auctioned dozens of casks, with each auction typically containing 6-12 casks as demand grows.

Since that first auction in 2014, several record-breaking cask auctions have captured headlines, raising awareness of the potential rewards from cask ownership. In April 2022, a 34-year-old cask of The Macallan sold for £1 million at auctioneer Whisky Hammer after its forgetful owner was reminded of its existence. That record was smashed in July 2022 when a cask of 1975 Ardbeg sold for £16 million.

These huge sums show how much appetite there is for rare and special whiskies. Cask 3, as the Ardbeg cask was called, was valuable not just because of its age but because most spirit of that age went into blends, creating a shortage of single malt of that vintage.

However, record sales are not the bread and butter of cask ownership. The growing number of whisky casks sold at auction shows that prices vary widely. Metacask, a marketplace for spirits-backed non-fungible tokens (NFTs), began auctioning a series of whisky cask NFTs with a unique work of digital art attached online in 2022. Initial auctions included a 1992 Springbank sherry hogshead that sold for US$165,000.

# New sources of return

Since 2008, low yields caused by ultra-loose central bank monetary policy have pushed investors to seek new sources of return. Alternative investments have expanded rapidly over the past 10 plus years both in terms of assets under management in alternatives such as hedge funds and private equity – data provider Preqin expects these to soar to US$17 trillion in 2025 from US$4 trillion in 2010 – and the range of investments on offer.

Investors are turning to less liquid assets, such as private debt, forestry and infrastructure. The violent swings in financial markets that have occurred since the Covid-19 pandemic and intensified due to the war in Ukraine have served to cement the trend towards diversification. Thanks to the modern, transparent approach adopted by responsible whisky cask brokerages to investment in the sector, whisky casks are now taking their place in the universe of alternative assets for the first time.

In common with other real assets, whisky casks, which typically have little or no correlation with global financial markets, can be a useful and profitable portfolio diversifier. However, as is the case with all specialised, illiquid investments, it is important to understand the market and the risks when investing in whisky casks. Responsible whisky casks brokers with a deep knowledge and appreciation of the whisky industry can help you to integrate whisky casks into your investment portfolio in a meaningful and productive way.

Innovations such as digitalisation and cryptocurrencies mean the way we invest and the assets we invest in are changing rapidly. Investors, particularly those from the millennial and Z generations, no longer automatically look to the banks and financial institutions that their parents trusted for investment advice. Providing a wide range of investors with professional and transparent access to whisky cask investment is part of that changing landscape and of a more diverse and often more open and democratic investment industry.

# 4 THE LIFE CYCLE OF A CASK

The physical cask is a crucial element in the production of single-malt whisky, creating many of the final spirit's flavours and imparting its colour. Single-malt whisky must be matured in oak casks, and most matures in ex-bourbon casks made from American oak (quercus alba), which account for 95% of all whisky casks, for all or most of its life span. European oak (quercus robur) is typically found in the sherry and wine casks that are used more and more both to mature some new-make single-malt whisky and for second maturation.

# The cooper's art

The cask begins life as an oak tree typically aged between 70 and 200, ideally standing tall and straight with no low-hanging branches. Because of the boom in demand for both whisky and bourbon, cooperages are sourcing wood from an ever-widening range of logging firms, which means lumber from several US states can end up in one US cooperage.

Before it arrives at the cooperage, the wood passes through a sawmill where the heartwood is cut into staves by sawing against the grain to prevent leakages when it is made into a barrel. At the cooperage, it is then either air or kiln dried. Air seasoning takes a minimum of a few months and sometimes several years.

The dried wood is planed to achieve similar widths and cut into longer trapezoid staves and shorter, straight pieces that are joined with dowels to create the barrel ends. From the shaped staves, the cooper must fashion a leak-proof cask. As the cask is formed, starting with a wide stave that will contain the bung hole, the wood is steamed for shaping and bound with temporary hoops.

The wood is then usually toasted for several minutes before the inside of the cask is set alight for a few seconds and charred. Charring is a legal requirement for bourbon casks, but toasting is not. When the cask has been tested for leaks, it is shipped to the distillery ready to be filled.

# Refilling casks

Bourbon must by law be matured in new barrels, ensuring a good supply of used barrels for the Scotch whisky industry. Used barrels are shipped to Scottish whisky distilleries either whole or broken down into staves to be filled with Scottish distillate, turning them into what is known as first-fill casks. Larger hogsheads are constructed from broken-down barrels with additional staves added.

The type of oak used in the cask and the way it was originally toasted and charred affect the flavours that it imparts, as does the number of times the cask is used. As a result, most whisky distilleries have clear cask preferences. Laphroaig, for example, uses only first-fill Maker's Mark casks. Other Scottish distilleries prefer casks from different bourbon producers, while some elect to use second, third or even fourth-fill casks in order not to overwhelm the spirit.

After several refills, a cask becomes depleted. However, it can be rejuvenated at the cooperage by shaving off its inner layer and toasting and charring it again.

# Sourcing non-bourbon casks

Demand for single-malt whisky that is matured or finished in sherry casks, and to a lesser extent in wine, port, madeira and rum casks, has increased exponentially. This has put pressure on the market for these casks, pushing prices up.

Most sherry now being produced is never drunk and is used to season casks for the secondary maturation of single-malt whisky. Clients can now order a cask from a sherry producer and specify whether it should be seasoned for 12 months, 24 months or longer.

This means that sourcing casks has become an important of part of distilleries', bottlers' and whisky cask brokers' expertise. Some sherries are preferred over others for finishing whisky, with Oloroso and Pedro Ximenez among the most popular. The Macallan and Dalmore favour Oloroso casks, for example.

Some individual sherry casks are better than others, and an 'off' cask can impart unwanted notes of sulphur. Used sherry casks also contribute differently to the whisky from seasoned casks. There isn't much activity in the wood of a 40-year-old sherry cask, but it will supply colour and flavour from the sherry that has been matured in it over the years. Therefore, this kind of cask is more appropriate for second maturation, while a seasoned cask, which will impart flavours from the wood as well as the sherry, is more typically used to mature new-make spirit.

# Cask provenance

Scotch whisky distilleries have also been experimenting with maturing their spirit in casks made from different kinds of oak. Bowmore, which is owned by Beam Suntory, has released a single malt finished in Japanese mizunara oak (quercus crispula) casks. As the different properties of different oaks become better understood, emphasis on provenance and *terroir* – already a topic for barley, peat and water – is increasing in the area of casks.

The growing emphasis on provenance is already discernible in the area of wine casks, which are increasingly used in single-malt whisky maturation. Some whisky companies are not just sourcing casks from specific vineyards but are asking for certain vintages. Often, however, naming rights are restricted with these wine casks, and it is not possible to name the château from which the cask came, only the region.

MANZANILLA

# 5

# HOW TO CHOOSE YOUR CASK

Whisky cask investment may seem to sit at the intersection between business and pleasure. Like other real assets such as works of art and fine wines, whisky casks are a serious investment that can provide excellent and stable returns, but they are also objects of desire. It is true that many whisky cask investors have a passion for the spirit within the cask, but it is worth remembering that not all do and over 90% of whisky casks that are bought as an investment aren't tasted until they are sold onwards.

Therefore, even among whisky enthusiasts, personal preference should play a relatively minor role in cask selection. Instead, the main criteria you should consider when choosing a cask are the distillery behind the cask and the naming rights it has granted, budget, time horizon and the qualities of the cask itself. You should also think about what you hope to achieve with the investment and how the cask fits into your wider investment portfolio.

# Naming rights

The distillery brand name is perhaps the single most important factor that will influence the future value of your cask. Brand value is derived not just from the distillery's heritage and reputation, but also from how it portrays itself in the market and its commitment to marketing. Casks from a distillery that is engaged in a major marketing and PR push are typically more valuable.

Braeburn Whisky tracks the average annual capital growth of casks from Scottish distilleries, and there can be a surprising amount of movement over a year. The 2021 list, for example, featured a new leader – Bunnahabhain, which knocked fellow Islay distillery Laphroaig from the top spot – and three new entrants: Mortlach, Glenallachie and Longmorn. Long a workhorse distillery producing spirit mainly for blend, Bunnahabhain has repositioned itself in the market as a producer of quality unpeated and peated single-malt Islay whisky.

In addition, there are marked performance differences among Scotland's six whisky regions of Campbeltown, Highlands, Islands, Islay, Lowlands and Speyside. In 2020, projected annual capital growth for the Islay region was 16.3%, while the equivalent figure for the Lowlands region was 9.8%.

Allied to the distillery brand name are the naming rights accorded to your cask. Ultimately, your cask will probably be bottled by an independent bottler, whether you sell it for bottling or a subsequent owner does. Because the bottler does not own the trademark, there are rules about how the distillery name is displayed on independent bottlings.

These rules mean that the words 'single malt whisky' must be bigger than on a proprietary bottling and that the distillery name must be less prominent than the bottler's name. However, some distilleries sell their spirit without these naming rights, which downgrades the desirability of the casks.

In addition, some casks are sold with trading names. For example, Highland Park sometimes sells its spirit as Whitlaw (distilled at Highland Park). To those in the know, such trading names may indicate a spirit from a particular era. When the Whitlaw spirit is bottled, the bottler can use the words "distilled at Highland Park" on the label, and so owning a cask of Whitlaw is effectively no different from owning a cask of Highland Park. However, a cask of Whitlaw may still be less desirable in the market than a cask of Highland Park as it has a more complex story that requires more explanation.

OLD STYLE SOUR MASH
BOURBON WHISKEY
5F14

# Cask quality and size

Aside from leaky or defective casks, there is no such thing as a wrong whisky cask. Single-malt scotch whisky must mature in oak casks. Usually, those casks have previously contained bourbon or sherry, though other kinds of casks such as wine or tequila casks are now used too. Some people consider certain casks to be more desirable than others because of the flavour or colour profile that they impart. There is a range of views and preferences. For you as an investor, the most important thing is therefore to understand what the cask brings to the spirit.

The quality of the workmanship on the cask is a consideration, though quality can mean different things to different people. Investors typically want a cask that is a good receptacle for holding liquid so that they don't lose too much to the angels. However, such a cask can be quite inactive. A bottler may prefer a cask that imparts lots of flavour, and those casks tend to be newer and more porous. You can't have both, so it's a question of balance.

Beyond that, the first variable when choosing your cask is size. There are three main types of cask: barrels (190-200 litres when full), hogsheads (225-250 litres) and butts (475-500 litres). Butts are ex-sherry, hogsheads can be ex-sherry or ex-bourbon, and barrels are usually ex-bourbon casks made from American oak.

Spirit matures more quickly in smaller casks, and the angel's share is greater, because there is more contact between the spirit and the wood. Investors therefore typically opt for hogsheads, which have a longer shelf life. However, if you want your spirit to mature more quickly you might choose a barrel.

No two casks are the same, and neither is the share the cask accords to the angels. It is therefore important to monitor the liquid level in your cask. Brokers will often describe your cask's contents in terms of the number of bottles it will fill rather than in litres, making it easier to position in the market. Typically, a barrel will fill 270-285 bottles, a hogshead 320-355 and a butt 675-715.

## Alcohol levels

Another important variable is the ABV of the spirit in the cask. Most Scottish distilleries put new-make spirit in the cask at 63.5%, which is generally considered to be the best ABV to ensure that extraction from the oak is not too rapid and the angel's share not too high. The minimum ABV at which single-malt Scotch whisky can be bottled is 40%. If you are buying a mature cask and planning to keep it for, say, 10 years, you must ensure that it has enough ABV to last that period and still be desirable to the next person when you sell it on.

A large part of a single-malt whisky's flavour and all its colour are derived from the oak in the cask or casks in which it matures, and the variables are manifold. Again, there is no right and wrong; it is a question of what you want to achieve. Different varieties of oak impart different flavours. The spirit that was in the cask previously also influences the flavour and colour that is achieved. Clearly, an ex-sherry cask will create a very different flavour and colour profile from an ex-bourbon cask. A professional broker can advise you on how best to make those variables work for you to create a premium spirit with market appeal.

# Budget and time horizon

With prices for new-make casks aged zero to two years starting at £1,500 to £3,000, there is a whisky cask for almost every budget. Typically, the newer and cheaper the cask, the longer the optimal holding period. Therefore, you must balance your budget and your time horizon when choosing your cask.

The optimal holding period for new-make casks and for emerging casks aged three to 10 years, is 15 years or more. This is not an investment for flippers; if you want to maximise the return on your investment in a new or emerging cask, you need to be in it for the long haul. If there is any risk you might need to exit early, an emerging cask is a better bet. As the minimum time new-make spirit must mature in casks to be considered whisky is three years, emerging casks can be sold for whisky and are therefore more liquid.

Intermediate casks aged 10-20 years have an optimal holding period of 10 years or more. Casks in this category can increase in value rapidly, because they become rarer and more sought after as equivalent casks are bottled.

Premium casks aged 20 years or more are the ideal choice if you have a bigger budget and are looking for a shorter-term investment with a potential upside of as much as 50% per year. These casks are rare and will ultimately be used for exclusive bottlings.

At the pinnacle of the whisky cask investment universe are blue-chip casks containing old and rare spirit from iconic distilleries. The age of these casks can vary, as can the optimal holding period. Exclusive blue-chip casks set auction records and are suitable for high-net-worth individuals looking for a single-malt whisky cask that is both a lucrative investment and a status symbol possession.

When investing in intermediate, premium or blue-chip casks, brokers often recommend buying just short of a significant birthday, such as 10, 12, 18, 21 or 25. For example, you could buy a 16-year-old cask and sell it at 20. The buyer might then bottle it as a 21-year-old, giving both parties ownership of the maturation process.

# Casks from new distilleries

A host of new whisky distilleries has opened in Scotland since 2010, with more in the pipeline and mothballed distilleries such as Brora and Port Ellen reopening. Some of them will be future stars, and some inevitably will not. Buying a cask from a new or reinvented distillery is riskier than buying from a long-established brand name with a consistent history but can bring rewards, especially for long-term investors.

As no one has tasted the matured single-malt spirit, buying a whisky cask from a new distillery will always be something of a leap of faith. To a lesser extent, the same is true of reopened distilleries. However, it is possible to assess the professional credentials of new and reopened distilleries and make a judgement that way.

The skill and knowledge levels of the distillery's backers and the people who work there, especially the master distiller, are perhaps the most important variable. But other factors, such as the distillery's commitment to marketing and PR, the equipment used, the processes, the cask management and even the look and feel of the distillery building can help brokers and investors to distinguish the likely future leaders from the also rans.

1988
12854
LAPHROAIG
ISLAY

# Autonomy of assets

Before investing in a whisky cask, you should ensure that you will have full control over the asset you are buying.

Whisky cask investment is not regulated by the UK's Financial Conduct Authority, which sometimes causes investor unease. However, the production, storage and sale of whisky is tightly controlled by HMRC regulations and by Scots law. In that sense, whisky casks are heavily regulated; there is no danger of a cask being misdescribed or of it disappearing.

Maturing whisky casks must be stored in the duty-suspended environment of an excise warehouse, and the spirit can only be released for bottling on payment to HMRC of alcohol duty. Warehouses and warehouse keepers must be registered with HMRC under the Warehousekeepers and Owners of Warehoused Goods Regulations (WOWGR) 1999.

Problems with establishing ownership can occur when a broker holds a whisky cask in a third-party warehouse on behalf of an investment client. The Scotch Whisky Association therefore advises you to ensure that you receive a legally binding bill of sale for your cask. This is your proof of ownership and should contain a detailed description of the whisky purchased and the cask, including the cask number, as well as WOWGR details and information on storage costs.

Some brokers have gone a step further to ensure clear lines of ownership. Braeburn Whisky has a client-use excise warehouse where its investment clients' casks are stored. In addition to receiving a bill of sale, Braeburn clients are listed on a ledger at the warehouse as owner of their casks. This ensures they have complete autonomy over their assets and are protected in the event of a business failure.

# 6 BUILDING WEALTH THROUGH WHISKY CASKS

As with any other investment, the secret to success with whisky cask investment is diversification. This applies both to your portfolio of whisky casks, if you decide to invest in more than one cask, and to the role whisky casks play in your wider investment portfolio. Sales of single-malt Scotch whisky are booming worldwide, but like any other industry, the Scotch whisky industry could be destabilised by unforeseen events. Whisky casks should only ever be one component in your long-term wealth-building strategy.

# A portfolio of casks

A single whisky cask can provide stable and attractive returns, allowing you to diversify your overall investment portfolio by investing in the only tangible asset that automatically increases in value as it ages due to the whisky maturation process. However, many investors prefer to spread their investment over a range of whisky casks, sometimes building their portfolios over a number of years.

Just like a portfolio of equities or bonds, a whisky cask portfolio can have a higher or lower risk profile. Some investors prefer to stick with well-known distillery brands, buying casks that are more expensive but have a more predictable value appreciation trajectory than casks from newer distilleries or ones that are less well-known. Others want to invest in casks from some of the whisky industry's many dynamic new players – or choose to combine old with new.

Some brokers offer a service whereby you can place a single investment into a range of, say, 10 casks. This allows you to spread your risk across regions, distilleries and cask age groups. These kinds of managed portfolios also appeal to the increasing number of wealth managers and family offices that are now looking to include whisky casks in their alternative investment allocations.

Beam

# Strike while the iron is hot

Because there is a shortage of whisky casks containing older single-malt spirit from well-known distilleries, you need to be prepared to act fast if you want to become the owner of an iconic cask. Premium and blue-chip casks sell quickly. Sometimes, they don't even make it on to the open market if a buyer is waiting who has registered their interest with a broker.

Decisiveness can also be important when it comes to re-selling your cask. If a broker approaches you with a good deal, you may need to act quickly, or the potential buyer could go elsewhere.

Because every cask is unique, each buying and selling opportunity is unique too and cannot be replicated. In that sense, investing in whisky casks is more like investing in works of art or other collectibles than investing in the stock market.

# Caring for your cask

An important advantage of investing in a cask through a broker is that they will care for your cask for you. For example, Braeburn Whisky looks after casks in its own client-use warehouse in Speyside. Your cask is likely to be better cared for at a proprietary facility such as this than at the distillery because there are fewer casks to look after and every cask is important, as it is someone's investment.

Monitoring your cask and completing any necessary repairs becomes more important as it ages, not least to ensure the ABV of the spirit does not dip below the desired level or below the minimum 40% ABV level for bottling as single-malt whisky. Older spirit evaporates less quickly because it is less volatile, but an annual weight gauge is recommended if the cask reaches an ABV in the mid-40s.

HEAVY TOAST
PX 2014
JACK ROSE

# Curating your cask

Investing in a whisky cask is not just about buying a cask and storing it until you are ready to sell. It is also about creating a unique and desirable spirit either to bottle yourself or to sell to an independent bottler.

A professional whisky cask broker can advise you on how best to maximise the value of the spirit in your cask. This is partly about determining the optimum length of time to leave the spirit in the cask. Your spirit becomes more valuable as it matures, but there is a curve, and so it's important to find the sweet spot. The timescale will also be determined by your investment objectives.

A broker can also help you to perfect the spirit in your cask by re-racking it. This is a process whereby the spirit is placed in a new cask for a period usually ranging from six months to three years for finishing. Single-malt whisky is often finished in ex-sherry casks, but wine, port, madeira, tequila, rum and mescal casks can be used.

The right finishing cask for your spirit depends on the distillate in the cask, the elements already imparted by the initial cask, and the flavour and colour profile that you want to achieve. It also depends on the casks that your whisky cask broker can offer. A good broker will have excellent relationships with cooperages, sherry producers and vineyards to source the best casks.

In addition, the best choice of finishing cask is governed by market trends and availability. Your whisky cask broker is not just there to sell you a cask. They can also help you create a spirit that is desirable to the independent bottlers who produce the whisky industry's finest bottlings, while not being in over-supply.

Another option is to split a cask for second maturation into smaller casks such as octaves. This allows the creation of two or more different whiskies from one cask.

## Cask-to-glass service

When it comes to monetising your whisky cask investment, there is a range of options. You may wish to sell the cask on to another investor or to an independent bottler. With demand for premium, speciality and rare whiskies booming, the market for well-curated casks that can provide independent bottlers with an outstanding, cask-strength single-malt spirit to bottle has become more liquid.

This same trend means that distilleries sometimes want to buy back casks of their own spirit for special releases. Alternatively, you may wish to bottle the spirit yourself and keep some or all of the bottles. A specialist whisky cask broker that is plugged into the market can offer you a cask-to-glass service that will enable you to monetise your asset quickly in the way that works best for you.

# FUTURE DIRECTIONS IN WHISKY CASK INVESTMENT

Whisky cask investment sits on the cusp of great change. Over the past decade, professional and transparent whisky cask brokerages have emerged, revolutionising a trade that was previously private and shrouded in secrecy.

Over the coming decade, investment in whisky casks is set to enter a new phase of development. Data on whisky casks sales are improving all the time, enabling more detailed and accurate analysis to support informed investment decisions. The BC20 index has helped investors to understand both how well whisky casks can perform compared to other investments and the added value that a managed portfolio of whisky casks can bring.

## Greater traceability

Spink expects whisky casks to constitute a vibrant and growing part of its collectables and lifestyle business over the coming years and, as whisky auctions become more common and brokers generate more sales, data will continue to improve. As a result, Braeburn Whisky's algorithm, which predicts future valuations, is becoming more precise all the time.

In a few years' time, the BC20 index will have to be rebalanced. The challenge of completing that process will shed further light on this expanding investment sector and the best ways to track it. Perhaps there will be further indices covering larger numbers of casks or specific regions. As nascent interest in whisky cask investment from wealth mangers and family offices grows, managed portfolios of casks may evolve into whisky cask investment funds.

Already, there is a regulated whisky investment fund in Sweden, though it invests in bottles not casks. The Single Malt Fund AB, which launched in 2019, is authorised by the Swedish Financial Supervisory Authority as an alternative investment fund (AIF) as defined by the EU directive on Alternative Investment Fund Managers.

The issue of autonomy of assets for investors in whisky casks has been largely solved by legally binding bills of sale and proprietary warehouse ledgers. New blockchain technology can provide further assurance and accountability. Non-fungible tokens (NFTs) can be used to establish provenance for assets such as whisky casks where there is no government-mandated register. Potentially, NFTs could also be used to track changes to the cask, such as re-racking, and to reflect the added-value benefits that might in some circumstances be included in a cask sale.

DISTILLERY
BOURBON WHISKEY
R.C. 53 DSP KY. 44
E21-7
12L03

# Provenance and sustainability

Provenance is all in the whisky industry and always has been. Over the last decade, however, the emphasis on the concept of *terroir* in whisky production has increased. Bruichladdich on Islay pioneered the use of locally grown barley in some of its spirit, with the result that barley is being grown again on Islay after a pause of many decades. The neighbouring farm distillery at Kilchoman has followed suit and taken matters a step further by instituting barley-to-bottle production.

The emphasis on provenance and *terroir* will only increase in years to come, not least because that is what millennial and generation Z consumers demand. This will affect physical casks too, as is already in evidence from the increasingly precise sourcing of sherry and wine casks in the Scotch whisky industry.

Right now, whisky cask provenance is all about where the cask has been before it comes to the whisky distillery. There is minimal emphasis on the provenance of the oak from which the cask is made, and it can be difficult to trace where the wood came from beyond placing it into broad-brush geographic categories such as American or European.

This could change, however. Latest scientific research is turning up ways to pinpoint the different qualities lent to whisky by different varieties of oak. This has the potential to open a whole new chapter in the *terroir* story, creating additional ways to distinguish casks.

With the price of wood on the increase – reports suggest the price of casks is doubling in the USA – greater sustainability could be part of that evolution towards more precise sourcing of wood. Again, this chimes with contemporary consumer sensibilities, and the growing emphasis on sustainable forestry is likely to be allied to sustainable whisky production, as energy costs rise and consumer awareness of climate change risks increases.

# Enhancing the dram in your glass

The aim of every whisky cask investor should not simply be to achieve a return on their investment but also to create a desirable finished product that someone will enjoy drinking. At a time when many Scotch whisky distilleries are dropping age statements on their core single-malt bottlings to meet demand, many of the best single-malt whiskies on the market are being produced by the independent bottlers that buy carefully curated casks from whisky cask brokers and investors.

The next five to ten years could therefore see an upsurge in unique and exciting bottlings, as whisky cask investors realise their assets. As investment in whisky casks grows, that trend – which is in tune with the overall direction of whisky enjoyment away from quantity and towards quality – is likely to intensify. A contributing factor to the expected upsurge in special bottlings is the large amount of spirit that independent bottlers purchased from distilleries during the Covid-19 pandemic when the 30% of whisky sales that happen in international airports disappeared overnight.

At the same time, the Scotch whisky industry is exploring new flavour avenues, deploying casks from new sources, such as Australian and other new-world vineyards. In due course, these innovations will be supplemented by spirit coming through from the many new distilleries established in Scotland over the past decade or so.

Along with new markets in Asia and South America, these new directions in terms of distillery names, provenance, flavour profile and sustainability support the future success of the Scotch whisky industry and the drive towards a higher-quality and more differentiated product. As the role of independent bottlers expands, they are becoming involved on the distillery side too, creating further variables. In 2002, independent bottler Signatory Vintage bought Edradour distillery, while in 2018 Glasgow-based bottler Hunter Laing filled the first cask at its new distillery Ardnahoe on Islay.

The net result of these changes is both interesting new casks for you to invest in and superlative drams for your glass. What could be better?

Slàinte mhath!

Thanks to

Makiyo, Kenzo, Hope 4Eva, Daisy, Maxi, Sylvie Chan, Olivier, Daniel L, Laarni, Steve S, Patrick, Niall, Sam G, KB, Mark S, JD, Lauren, Daniel C, Erika, Zorab, Adam, all at Forsyth's, Uncle Ricky, Alberto and the magic rabbits, Greg and Dimitra, Raul, Luis, Xavier, Miriam, Mayor Worster, Monica, Leah, Alvaro, all the Pink Ladies, all at Teaghlach holdings and the past whisky masters of before who made it all possible some of whom are John Walker, Andrew Usher, The Grants both Glenfiddich and Glenfarclas, Roderick Kemp, Morrison family and so many others we salute you all.

# APPENDICES

# The distilleries of Scotland

From the leafy corners of Speyside to the wind-swept shores of Islay, Scotland's distilleries are home to the world's most valuable casks. Each individual cask is unique, the product of the distinctive whisky-making traditions that define the special character and history of every distillery.

With over 130 malt and grain distilleries, Scotland has the greatest concentration of whisky production in the world. The distilleries are located across six regions: Speyside, Highlands, Lowlands, Campbeltown, Islay and Islands. Although geography is important, it is the individual 'house' style, the whisky making heritage of the distillery and, above all, the casks that give each single malt its distinctive qualities.

This appendix includes a list of distilleries renowned for producing some of the finest casks in Scotland.

# ANNANDALE

*Northfield, Annan DG12 5LL, UK*

After decades in abeyance, the Annandale distillery has now sprung back and is recovering the lost traditions of Lowland single malt at the hands of its owners Prof David Thomson and Teresa Church. First established in 1836 by George Donald and later bought by Johnnie Walker in 1893, it closed down again in 1924, before beginning distillation again and broaching its first cask of the new era in 2017. Annandale seeks a common flavour profile for both its peated and unpeated expressions, using largely sherry-seasoned casks and STR casks (shaved, toasted & re-charred) for its releases.

- The Founders Selection range explores the rarest casks.
- Robert Burns was a regular visitor to the distillery.
- Recovering the traditions of Lowland whisky making.

Region:
Lowlands

Year Founded:
1836

Status:
Operational / Active

Owner:
Annandale Distillery Company

Capactity:
N/A

"The re-awakening of the Annandale Distillery means that fine Single Malt now flows again from Dumfries and Galloway."

# ARDBEG

*Port Ellen, Islay PA42 7EA, UK*

It's not often that you find a distillery with as many awards as Ardbeg. Purchased by Glenmorangie in 1997, Ardbeg has grown in popularity ever since and has become a successful global brand with an incredible reputation for creating the smokiest malts in the industry. While the distillation process has changed slightly since Glenmorangie took over, the team attributes much of the character to the distillery itself, its location, and the rich history behind it.

- 1 wash (18,000 L); 1 spirit (17,000 L).
- Creates the smokiest malt in the industry.
- Held the crown for Distillery of the Year three years running.

Region:
Islay

Year Founded:
1815

Status:
Operational / Active

Owner:
The Glenmorangie Co

Capacity:
2.4 Million Litres / year

"Ardbeg has become one of Scotland's premier distilleries. Its exceptional whisky is one of the ultimate expressions of a peated single malt."

# ARDMORE

*Kennethmont, Huntly AB54 4NH, UK*

The Ardmore distillery sits at the highest point of the Northern railway line, 600 feet above sea level. Taking its water from the nearby Knockandy Spring, the distillery is known for its peated single malt and as a base for the famous Teacher's Highland Cream, a smooth blended whisky variety that has been in demand for over a hundred years. Ardmore malts are generally known for their sweetly smoked peat flavour base. The distillery was first built in 1898 and was expanded in 1955 when two more stills were added to the operation, which currently has four wash stills and four spirit stills.

- Non-chill filtered whisky.
- Ex-Bourbon casks.
- Water sourced from Knockandy spring.

Region:
Highlands

Year Founded:
1898

Status:
Operational / Active

Owner:
Beam Suntory

Capacity:
5.5 Million Litres / year

"A whisky that soars to new heights of flavour, like the golden eagle that adorns its emblem".

# BENRINNES

*Aberlour, Banffshire, AB38 9NN, UK*

The distillery sits at the foot of the Ben Rinnes mountains, from where it takes its name. Once famous for its unusual partial triple distillation process, which it used until 2007, the whisky it produces remains a prized base for many popular blends, including Johnny Walker. Active since 1826, Benrinnes, or 'Lyne of Ruthrie' as it was called at the time, was founded by Peter McKenzie who saw the distillery through a subsequent flood and rebuilding. The distillery, now owned by the spirit giant Diageo, is equipped with two wash and four spirit stills.

- Triple distillation delivers a unique flavour for older casks.
- Distinctive heavy stone brick warehouses.
- Substantial number of independent bottlings.

Region:
Speyside

Year Founded:
1834

Status:
Operational/ Active

Owner:
Diageo

Capactity:
3.6 Million Litres / year

"A historic Speyside distillery that produces a light and aromatic single malt."

# BEN NEVIS

*Lochy Bridge, Fort William PH33 6TJ, UK*

The Ben Nevis distillery sits at the base of Britain's highest mountain of the same name. As one of the first distilleries to become legally established in Scotland, Ben Nevis took advantage of the whisky boom in the 1800s before many of its competitors entered the market. Ben Nevis has four stills, two wash and two spirit. Together they produce about 2 million litres of full-bodied, slightly sweet spirit each year. Ben Nevis mainly uses sherry and bourbon casks to mature their iconic spirit. The casks contribute to the bold and heavy character that Ben Nevis is known for.

- A bold spirit with an exceptionally fruity and rich, chewy texture.
- Original site of "blending at birth" maturation method.
- Booming visitor centre with an immersive whisky experience.

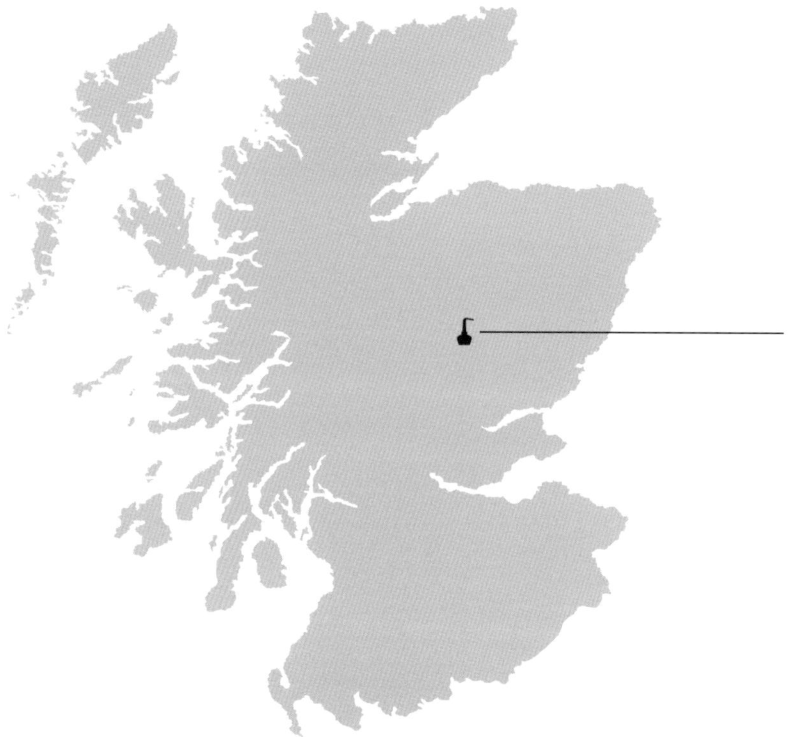

Region:
Highlands

Year Founded:
1825

Status:
Operational / Active

Owner:
Nikka

Capactity:
2 Million Litres / year

"Ben Nevis has a rich history and an even brighter future."

# BOWMORE

*School St, Bowmore, Isle of Islay PA43 7JS, UK*

Bowmore, the oldest distillery on Islay, was founded in 1779 by David Simpson. Using a mixture of peated and unpeated barley gives Bowmore a more subtle, smoky profile than some other whiskies from Islay, making it more approachable and balanced. The distillery sits on the shore of Loch Indaal in the centre of the town of Bowmore, from which the distillery takes its name. The distillery is proud to have won more awards than any other Scottish distillery since its inception, firmly cementing its place as a legend of Scotch whisky.

- Houses oldest existing warehouse in Scotland (Vault No. 1).
- Uses original warehouses and water sources since opening in 1779.
- In-house floor maltings keep traditional distillation alive.

Region:
Islay

Year Founded:
1779

Status:
Operational / Active

Owner:
Beam Suntory

Capactity:
2 Million Litres / year

"Every Bowmore is a pleasure to drink and a good cask choice for any portfolio."

# BRUICHLADDICH

*Isle of Islay PA49 7UN, UK*

Bruichladdich, meaning "raised beach", sits on the island of Islay off the coast of western Scotland. The distillery is known for using barley only grown in Scotland, some of which is organic. Bruichladdich focuses on their local community, employing about 80 people from the area and working with local farmers to expertly craft their whisky. Bruichladdich's annual output of 1.5 million litres is thanks to the four stills on-site. All whiskies released under the Bruichladdich brand are unpeated, however Bruichladdich is also known for creating the world's most heavily peated expression, under their Octomore brand.

- Preserves superior flavour and mouthfeel with no chill-filtration.
- 100% Islay barley for whisky-making.
- Striving to become 100% "green" by 2025.

Region:
Islay

Year Founded:
1881

Status:
Operational / Active

Owner:
Rémy Cointreau

Capacity:
1.5 Million Litres / year

"This eco-conscious, progressive Hebridean distiller is leading the way in contemporary single malt."

# BUNNAHABHAIN

*Port Askaig, Isle of Islay, PA46 7RR, UK*

Bunnahabhain means "mouth of the river" in Gaelic. It's a fitting name as the Islay distillery sits at the mouth of the Margadale Spring. The Margadale is a unique component of the whisky at Bunnahabhain, as it doesn't have the peated flavour of other water sources in the Islay region. Though the distillery is in the Islay region, which is traditionally associated with peated spirit, Bunnahabhain is known for having an array of unpeated single malts. However, after the most recent takeover in 2003, the master distiller reintroduced some traditional peated expressions to join the whisky lineup.

- Unpeated expressions are non-traditional for the Islay region.
- Recent £10.5 million investment on upgrades to the distillery.
- Uses pure spring water from Islay for distillation.

Region:
Islay

Year Founded:
1883

Status:
Operational / Active

Owner:
Burn Steward Distillers

Capacity:
3.2 Million Litres / year

"There's nothing like a dram of Bunna' to raise the spirits!"

# CAOL ILA

*Port Askaig, Isle of Islay PA46 7RL, UK*

The Caol Ila distillery is situated on the east coast of the historic island of Islay with stunning views across to the Paps of Jura. Caol Ila translates as 'The Sound of Islay', which is fitting for the style of whisky produced here. Enthusiasts enjoy Caol Ila's mostly traditional peated spirit with hints of maritime and exotic fruits. Although peated, Caol Ila spirit offers a delicate smoky profile, which is more subtle than other distilleries on the Island. Today, Caol Ila is home to 6 stills in total, 3 wash and 3 spirit, and outputs around 6.5 millions litres of spirit per year.

- Largest whisky-producing capacity on Islay.
- A significant component in Johnnie Walker Blend.
- Only 15% of the spirit is dedicated to the single malt market.

Region:
Islay

Year Founded:
1846

Status:
Operational / Active

Owner:
Diageo

Capactity:
6.5 Million Litres / year

"Caol Ila is a go-to cask for Islay single malts. We're constantly impressed by the quality of the whisky coming from this distillery."

# CRAIGELLACHIE

*Hill St, Craigellachie, Aberlour AB38 9ST, UK*

The name Craigellachie means 'rocky hill', which perfectly describes the distillery's position on a hill overlooking the confluence of the rivers Fiddich and Spey. Located in the heart of Speyside, the Craigellachie Distillery sits next to some of Scotland's premiere distilleries. However, since 1891 Craigellachie has followed its own distinctive path, creating a spirit famed for its robust character and distinctive pineapple aroma thanks to a firm commitment to a unique production process.

- Water sourced from underground Blue Hill spring.
- Rare single malt releases, adding value to casks.
- Unique malting process using 'sulphurous' steam.

Region:
Speyside

Year Founded:
1891

Status:
Operational

Owner:
Bacardi

Capactity:
4 Million Litres / year

"When it comes to Speyside single malt,
it's hard to beat a Craigellachie."

# DUFFTOWN

*Church St, Dufftown, Keith AB55 4BR, UK*

Located in the town with the highest concentration of distilleries in the world, the Dufftown distillery is nestled in the leaves of the Spey valley. As part of the Diageo group, the Dufftown spirit plays a key role in some of the world's most famous blends, with only 3% making it to single malt bottlings. Because of this, Dufftown's place as a single malt expression has been a secret kept by the most devout enthusiasts. A handful of official bottlings, including a few under The Singleton line, have provided whisky lovers with a taste of Dufftown's magic and created a following for its nectar.

- The distillery occupies an old grain mill.
- Distinctive 'pear-shaped' stills.
- Spirit used in the world's most popular blends.

Region:
Speyside

Year Founded:
1896

Status:
Operational / Active

Owner:
Diageo

Capacity:
6 Million Litres / year

"The rare arrival of a single malt from this historic distillery is always a moment to celebrate."

# GLENFARCLAS

*Ballindalloch, Banffshire AB37 9BD, UK*

Glenfarclas, which means 'valley of the green grass' is one of the most picturesque distilleries in Speyside. It also has the distinction of being one of the last family-owned whiskies in Scotland. The single malt, carefully crafted by six generations of the Grant family, is full-bodied and fruity, matured exclusively in sherry seasoned casks. The distillery has approximately 68,000 casks maturing on site in traditional dunnage warehouses, with stock from 1953 to the current year. The three wash stills and three spirit stills are directly fired with gas, using a traditional methodology.

- Family owned for almost 150 years.
- Traditional pagoda distillery roof.
- Exceptional stock of old single malt.

Region:
Speyside

Year Founded:
1836

Status:
Operational / Active

Owner:
J & G. Grant

Capactity:
4 Million Litres / year

"The long years of dedication to crafting the best single malt can be savoured with every sip. Let's raise a glass to the Grant family."

# GLENFIDDICH

*Dufftown, Keith AB55 4DH, UK*

Glenfiddich derives from *Gleann Fhiodhaich* meaning "valley of the deer", which is referenced in the famous stag logo that proudly graces all its bottles. Founded in 1886 by William Grant, Glenfiddich has now become the world's best-selling single malt with a capacity of 13,000,000 litres of spirit from its 31 distinctively-shaped "swan neck" copper pot stills. All stills are handmade and Glenfiddich employs a team of craftsmen to maintain them. Glenfiddich malts are laid down in a variety of rum, ex-bourbon and sherry casks all tended by one of the last remaining on-site cooperages in Scotland.

- Pioneered single malt with first release in 1963 for the US market.
- Managed by the fifth-generation of the Grant family.
- Water sourced from the nearby Robbie Dhu springs.

Region:
Speyside

Year Founded:
1886

Status:
Operational / Active

Owner:
William Grant & Sons

Capactity:
13 Million Litres / year

"Famous worldwide, this single malt giant continues to explore its rich heritage with each new release."

# GLENKINCHIE

*Pencaitland, Tranent EH34 5ET, UK*

Sometimes known as 'the Edinburgh Malt' due to its close proximity to the capital, the Glenkinchie Distilery has been under the radar for decades, but is now widely recognized for its award-winning  Lowland single malt. The distillery has just two stills, one spirit and one wash—however, the wash still is reputedly the largest in Scotland. Glenkinchie, now owned by spirit giant Diageo, is one of the Four Corner distilleries of the Johnnie Walker brand experience tour.

- Famous for its Lowland Garden.
- Unique shape of stills creates a distinct spirit.
- New, refurbished visitor centre.

Region:
Lowlands

Year Founded:
1837

Status:
Operational / Active

Owner:
Diageo

Capactity:
1.7 Million Litres / year

"It's no mystery why this is the favourite Lowland distillery of many whisky connoisseurs."

# GLENLIVET

*Ballindalloch AB37 9DB, UK*

Nestled in the picturesque Livet valley in Speyside, The Glenlivet was founded in 1824 by George Smith. From this date on, only this Scotch has had the right to call itself 'The Glenlivet' (a name derived from the Gaelic for "smooth flowing valley"). The distillery draws water from Josie's Well and other springs a short distance from the distillery. Glenlivet's stills are lantern shaped with long, narrow necks, all of which helps to produce a light-tasting spirit. The distillery has 7 wash stills, each with a capacity of 15,000 litres, and 7 spirit stills with a total capacity of 10,000 litres.

- Light and delicate spirit thanks to taller stills.
- The Glenlivet is the best-selling malt whisky in the USA.
- Used in the production of brands like Chivas Regal.

Region:
Speyside

Year Founded:
1824

Status:
Operational / Active

Owner:
Pernod Ricard

Capactity:
6 Million Litres / year

"Often considered 'the definitive Speyside malt', The Glenlivet provides a memorable dram to enjoy."

# GLENLOSSIE

*Thomshill, Elgin, IV30 8ST, UK*

Glenlossie is a quiet, mostly unknown distillery in the Speyside region. But despite its "undercover attitude" – Glenlossie's whisky is made with an uncommon use of purifiers that creates an almost creamy and slightly oily character that is extremely delightful to the palate. It is also known for its burst of fruit and grassy flavours, making Glenlossie a one-of-a-kind dram. Glenlossie also plays host to another Diageo distillery, Mannochmore, found on the same property. The pair are located near the river Lossie, just south of Elgin. Though the two distilleries produce vastly different flavour profiles, they share an on-site bonded warehouse home to around 200,000 casks.

- Focused on eco-friendly techniques.
- Home of a unique Dark Grains Plant.
- Extremely limited official releases make independent bottlings very desirable .

Region:
Speyside

Year Founded:
1876

Status:
Operational / Active

Owner:
Diageo

Capactity:
1.1 Million Litres / year

"The occasional arrival of a Glenlossie is a cause for celebration."

# THE GLENROTHES

*Rothes, Aberlour AB38 7AA, UK*

Based in the Speyside town of Rothes, overlooking the town's cemetery, The Glenrothes distillery has been producing its delicate, rich and elegant single malt since 1879, when it was founded by James Stuart & Co. A traditional, no-frills distillery, The Glenrothes produces a variety of single malt, bottled at natural colour and matured exclusively in sherry-seasoned casks sourced from Jerez in Spain.

- Part of The Edrington Group portfolio.
- Tall copper stills create a light and fruity spirit.
- The estate is next to the Burn of Rothes, its own source of water.

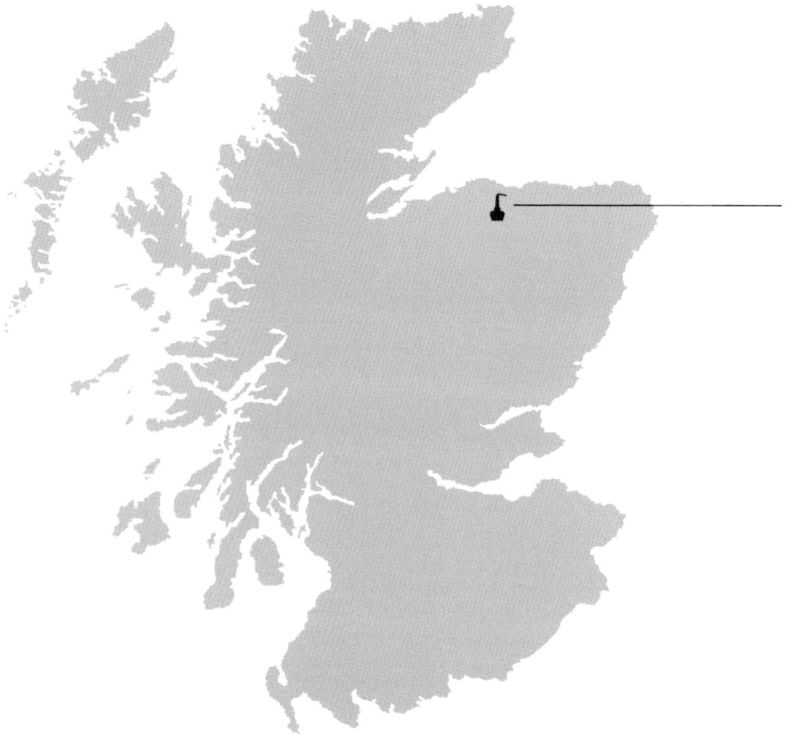

Region:
Speyside

Year Founded:
1879

Status:
Operational / Active

Owner:
The Edrington Group

Capacity:
N/A

"The long tradition and dedication to single malt can be tasted in every dram."

# HIGHLAND PARK

*Holm Rd, Kirkwall KW15 1SU, UK*

One of two distilleries on Orkney, Highland Park Distillery stands proudly in the island's remote and remarkable landscape with a rich history of whisky production stretching back to 1798. Highland Park uses Hebridean peat from the Hobbister Moor where, due to the unforgiving weather, no trees grow. These conditions give the peat a distinct floral character from the low-lying plants and heather, unlike any other in Scotland. Turning the malt by hand delivers the aromatic smokiness Highland Park is known for and continues a tradition which most distilleries have chosen to industrialise.

- Part of Edrington's premium spirit lineup, alongside The Macallan.
- It is the north-most distillery in the world.
- Uses cool maturation for a higher alcohol content and hand-turned malt for a unique smokiness.

Region:
Islands

Year Founded:
1798

Status:
Operational / Active

Owner:
Edrington

Capacity:
2.5 Million Litres / year

"Highland Park has gone from strength to strength to now become one of the best distilleries in Scotland."

# JURA

*Craighouse, Isle of Jura PA60 7XT, UK*

The remote island of Jura is located off the west coast of Scotland. It's doesn't have much to shout about – just one road and one pub. But this small, unassuming island does host one of the world's most iconic distilleries. Jura has built their brand up in the eyes of enthusiasts with its wide range of single malt expressions: in the last decade alone, Jura's single malt sales figures have skyrocketed an impressive 150%. The smooth and delicate flavour that Jura is known for is thanks to some of the tallest stills in the industry, giving the spirit its pure character.

- One of Scotland's most remote distilleries.
- Unusually tall stills provide a purer spirit.
- Own water source at Loch a'Bhaile Mhargaidh.

Region:
Islands

Year Founded:
1810

Status:
Operational / Active

Owner:
Whyte & Mackay

Capactity:
2.4 Million Litres / year

"The Jura Distillery produces some of our favourite expressions of fine, single malt."

# LAPHROAIG

*Isle of Islay PA42 7DU, UK*

Laphroaig, which means "broad hollow by the bay", was founded by two cattle farming brothers in 1815. The distillery rests in the Islay region and is known for making whisky with a strong, peaty flavour. The distillery uses seven stills – three wash and four spirit. Its global popularity as a single malt means that Laphroaig has a capacity of 3.3 million litres annually with about 70% dedicated to single malt expressions. With its traditional approach and extraordinary selection of bottlings, there's no doubt that Laphroaig has become a legendary player among Scotland's distilleries.

- Water source: The Kilbride Dam.
- Only 'legal' whisky available in the US during prohibition.
- Keeps tradition alive with hand-cut peat and malting floors.

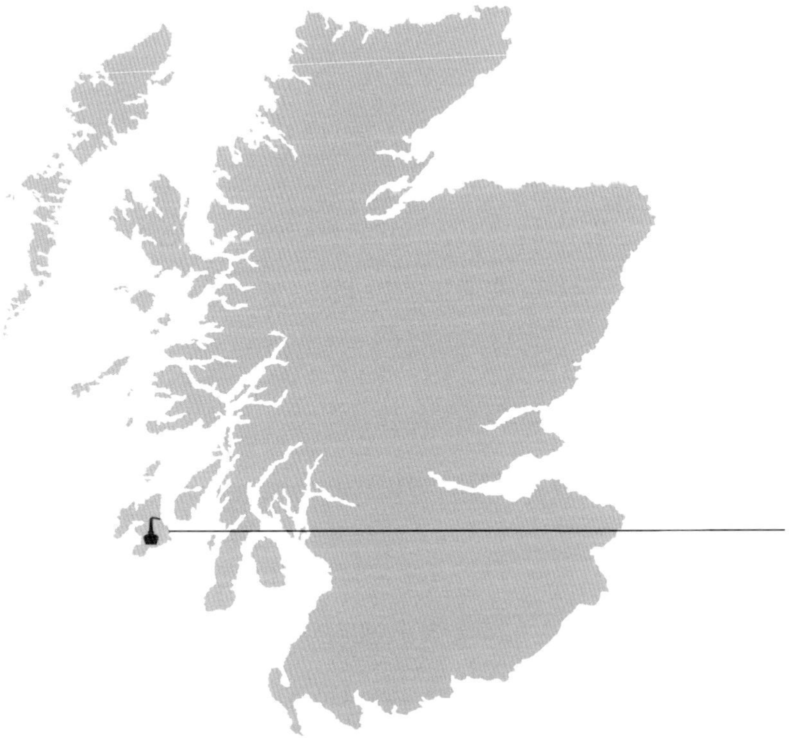

Region:
Islay

Year Founded:
1815

Status:
Operational / Active

Owner:
Beam Suntory

Capactity:
3.3 Million Litres / year

"Laphroaig whisky continues to divide opinion. But we are big fans of its intense, smoky flavours."

# LINKWOOD

*Knockando, Aberlour AB38 7RP, UK*

Linkwood has 6 stills (3 wash and 3 spirit),which are responsible for producing the sweet, perfumed spirit with grassy notes that the distillery is famous for. By clinging to tradition and, arguably, the presence of some old cobwebs at the distillery, Linkwood has held true to its roots after almost two centuries of operation. Today, Linkwood's spirits make up a key part of the prestigious blends under the Diageo name, including Johnnie Walker. Of the 3.5 million litres produced annually, only 1-2% of the spirit from Linkwood makes its way to the world of single malts.

- Iconic flavour profile with sweeter, perfumed spirit.
- Star component of Diageo's blends, including Johnnie Walker.
- Recently underwent a £5million expansion because of increasing demand.

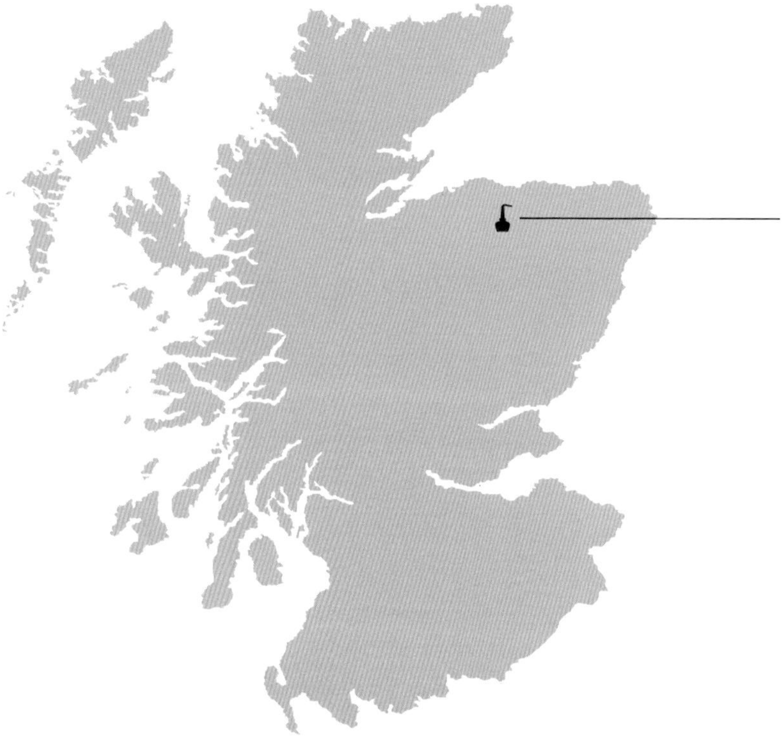

Region:
Speyside

Year Founded:
1821

Status:
Operational / Active

Owner:
Diageo

Capactity:
3.5 Million Litres / year

"Linkwood quietly produces one of Scotland's finest single malts. A highly-prized cask for investors."

# THE MACALLAN

*Easter Elchies, Aberlour AB38 9RX, UK*

Renowned worldwide for producing a highly select and premium spirit, that matures almost exclusively in fine sherry casks, The Macallan's reputation for being the best is hard-earned. The new state-of-the art distillery designed by the Richard Rogers studio is a masterpiece of beautiful architecture designed to match the elite style of the whisky it creates. But don't be fooled by its "showy" appearance; the distillery is still crafting world-class whisky at an astonishing rate of 15 million litres each year from its 12 wash stills and 24 spirit stills.

- Consistently sells for record prices at auction.
- Uniquely famous for small stills that create a profound flavour.
- Uses only hand-selected Sherry seasoned casks, crafted according to Macallan specifications.

Region:
Speyside

Year Founded:
1824

Status:
Operational

Owner:
Edrington Group

Capactity:
15 Million Litres / year

"Owning a cask of The Macallan is the pinnacle of any whisky cask investor's journey."

# MORTLACH

*Dufftown, Keith, Banffshire, AB55 4AQ, UK*

The Mortlach distillery was the first legal distillery in Dufftown, located in the Speyside region. Now, it's known as "The Beast of Dufftown" due to its bold flavour profile in a region generally known for gentler whiskies. The distillery prides itself on its unique 2.81 distillation process, which is used exclusively at Mortlach. Until recently, a cask of Mortlach's single malt whisky was almost impossible to come by. Most of what Mortlach distilled was reserved for the renowned Johnnie Walker blends. Now, independent bottlings of Mortlach are highly desired among whisky enthusiasts because of the distillery's growing popularity in the single malt whisky scene.

- The most unique 2.81 distillation process in the industry.
- First legal distillery in Dufftown.
- Until recently, used almost exclusively as part of the prestigious Johnnie Walker blend.

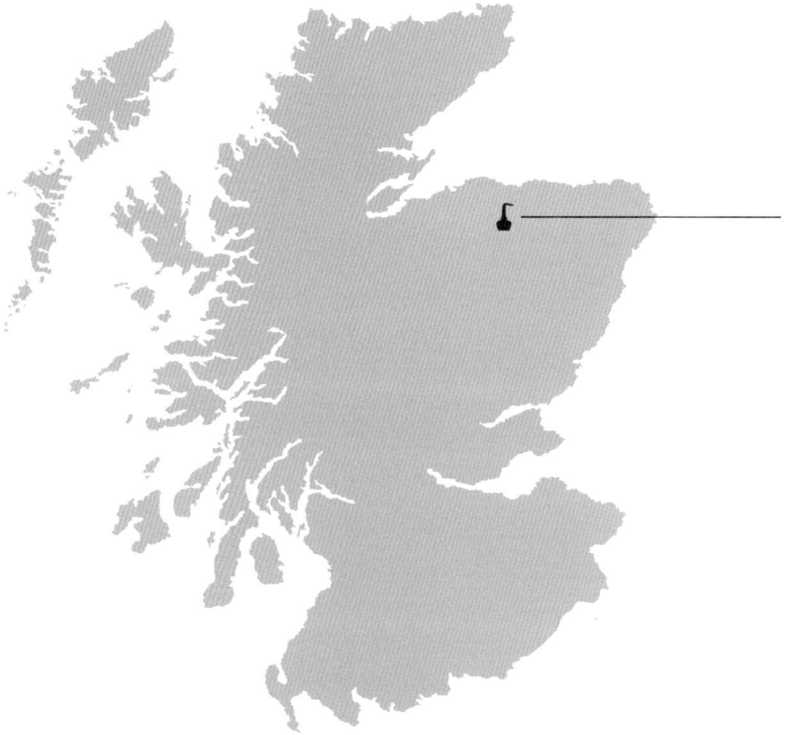

Region:
Speyside

Year Founded:
1823

Status:
Operational / Active

Owner:
Diageo

Capacity:
3.8 Million Litres / year

"This whisky features in some of the world's best blends. But always be on the look-out for its single malt expression."

# SPRINGBANK

*Campbeltown PA28 6ET, UK*

Located on the picturesque west coast of Scotland and first established in 1828, Springbank is one of the last surviving producers of single malt in Campbeltown; a whisky making region that once had over thirty active distilleries but is now Scotland's smallest. With 1 wash and 2 spirit stills the distillery produces three types of peated and unpeated malt whisky that it bottles under three distinct brands. Springbank is currently the only Scottish distillery to carry out every step in the whisky-making process, from malting the barley to bottling the spirit, using a traditional malting floor that provides 100% of their distillate.

- 100% of the barley comes from traditional floor malting methods.
- The only distillery in Scotland to produce three distinct malts at one site.
- Owned by the same family for 5 generations.

Region:
Campbletown

Year Founded:
1828

Status:
Operational / Active

Owner:
J&A Mitchell and Co.

Capactity:
750,000 Litres / year

"Known as the 'whisky drinker's whisky', Springbank is definitely a dram for connoisseurs."

# TALISKER

*Carbost, Isle of Skye IV47 8SR, UK*

Set on the shores of Loch Harport, Talisker is the oldest distillery on the Isle of Skye. Producing a spicy, slightly peated single malt, it is said that the salty winds of the Atlantic play a part in the distinctive taste of a Talisker. The distillery has five stills, three spirit and two wash. The curious loop shape of the 'swan neck' lyne pipes take the vapour from the stills to the worm tubs so some of the alcohol already condenses before it reaches the cooler. Additionally, the water used for production, from Cnoc nan Speireag (Hawk Hill), flows over peat which adds additional complexity to the whisky.

- The favourite dram of Robert Louis Stevenson.
- Casks warehoused next to the ocean.
- Part of the Classic Malts of Scotland collection.

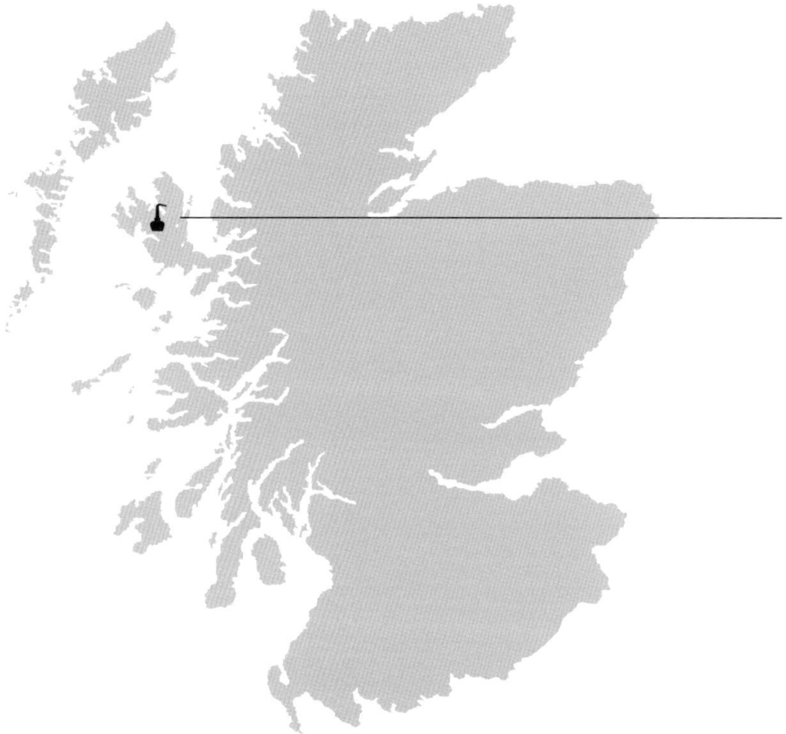

Region:
Islands

Year Founded:
1830

Status:
Operational / Active

Owner:
Diageo

Capacity:
3.5 Million Litres / year

"From the rugged shores of Skye to the smooth liquid in your glass, Talisker produces a whisky of fascinating complexity."

# TAMDHU

*Knockando, Aberlour AB38 7RP, UK*

Tamdhu, meaning "little dark hill" in Gaelic, sits in the heart of Scotch whisky production. Tamdhu perfectly encapsulates the true light and fruity character of a Speyside whisky by exclusively using Oloroso sherry casks to mature their award-winning whisky. Casks go through a six-year process of drying and seasoning before ever making their appearance at Tamdhu. Today, Tamdhu has 6 stills in total and produces around 2.5 million litres of spirit annually. Tamdhu has always sourced their Oloroso sherry casks from Spain and it is the only Scotch distillery to use Saladin boxes for their malting process.

- Exclusively uses sherry casks from Spain during maturation.
- Won the World's Best Single Cask Whisky award in 2020.
- Only Scotch distillery to use Saladin boxes today.

Region:
Speyside

Year Founded:
1897

Status:
Operational / Active

Owner:
Ian MacLeod Distillers, Ltd.

Capactity:
2.5 Million Litres / year

"There are few things finer in life than a dram of Tamdhu. These exceptional sherry casks are highly prized by investors."

# TULLIBARDINE

*Blackford, Auchterarder PH4 1QG, UK*

The Tullibardine distillery stands proudly in the village of Blackford – the gateway to the Highlands. For decades this independent, family-owned distillery has been producing handcrafted, single malt whisky. Although located in a spot that has been distilling for centuries, the distillery in its current incarnation began operating in 1947, using water drawn from the nearby Ochil Hills, famous for the purity of its clear springs. With four stills (two wash and two spirit), the whisky from Tullibardine, matured in a variety of ex-bourbon, sherry-seasoned and wine casks, is renowned for its well-balanced flavour.

- Owned by an independent spirits company since 2011.
- Wide range of quality casks.
- Water drawn from nearby spring.

Region:
Highlands

Year Founded:
1947

Status:
Operational / Active

Owner:
Terroirs Distillers

Capactity:
2.7 Million Litres / year

"An exceptional wood policy and handcrafted approach makes every dram from Tullibardine worth experiencing."